The life cycle of a
Crab

Ruth Thomson

WAYLAND

First published in 2008 by Wayland,
a division of Hachette Children's Books

Copyright © Wayland 2008

Wayland
338 Euston Road
London NW1 3BH

Wayland Australia
Level 17/207 Kent Street
Sydney, NSW 2000

Editor: Clare Lewis
Designer: Simon Morse
Consultant: Michael Scott OBE, B.Sc

Photographs: 14 Frank Greenaway/DK/Getty Images;
cover (cr), 13, 23br Image Quest 3-D/NHPA; 6 Dave
King/DK/Getty Images; 17 Frank Lane Picture
Agency/Corbis; 21 Renee Morris/Alamy;
12 Papilio/Alamy;8 Steve Stone/
iStockphoto; 7, 19 Roy Waller/NHPA
1, 2, 4, 7, 9, 10, 11, 15, 16, 18, 20, 22,
23tr, 23tl, 23bl naturepl.com

British Library Cataloguing in
Publication DataThomson, Ruth
    The life cycle of a crab. - (Learning
    about life cycles)
    1. Crabs - Life cycles - Juvenile literature
    I. Title
    595.3'86156
    ISBN-13: 978-0-7502-5597-4

Printed and bound in China

Wayland is a division of Hachette Children's
Books, an Hachette Livre UK company
www.hachettelivre.co.uk

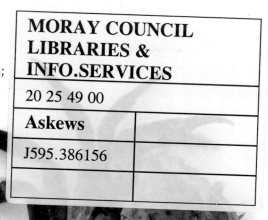

Contents

Crabs live here

Crabs usually live in the sea, by sandy or rocky seashores. They hide during the day. At night, they come out to feed.

What is a crab?

A crab has a soft body, which is protected by a hard, shiny shell. It has five pairs of **jointed** legs. The front two legs have claws. The others are used for walking and swimming.

Common shore crab ▼

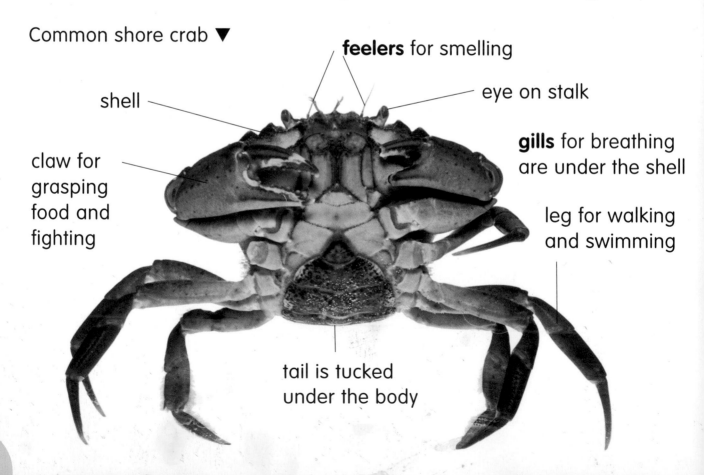

feelers for smelling

eye on stalk

shell

gills for breathing are under the shell

claw for grasping food and fighting

leg for walking and swimming

tail is tucked under the body

The crab's dark blotchy shell
is almost the same colour
as the rocks where it lives.
This makes it hard to see.

Finding a mate

In summer, a male crab finds a female to **mate** with.

eggs

The female lays thousands of tiny eggs.
She carries them about tucked under her
body. They are fixed on to stiff **bristles**.

Larvae

When the eggs are ready to **hatch**, the mother sits in the water and uncurls her tail. The eggs then float away.

4
months

The eggs hatch into tiny **larvae** with long spines that help them float. The sea carries them to new homes. Many larvae are eaten by fish and jellyfish on the way.

Moulting

A **larva's** skin cannot stretch.
As its body grows, the larva's skin splits
and falls off. This is called **moulting**.
It has a new skin underneath.

The larva moults several times. It changes shape and becomes a small crab. It grows too heavy to float and sinks to the seabed.

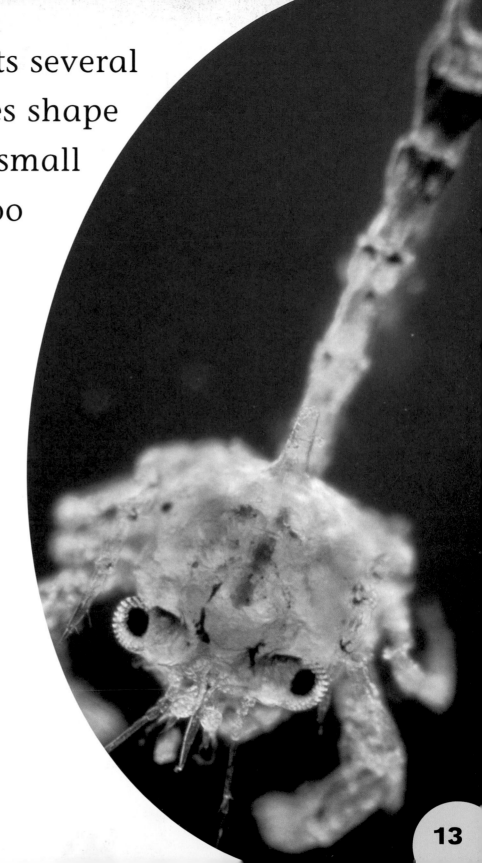

Feeding

A crab feeds on shellfish such as mussels and clams. It crushes their shells with one claw and scoops out the inside with the other.

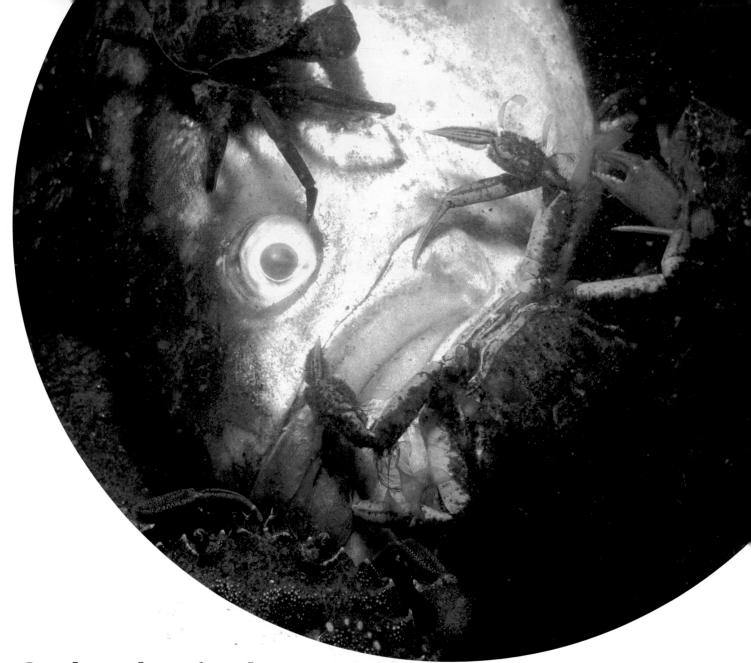

Crabs also feed
on dead animals such as fish,
starfish or other crabs.

New shells

A crab keeps growing for several years.
Its shell cannot stretch. As its body
grows, the crab **moults** and grows
a new shell.

old shell

new shell

At first, this new shell is soft.
The crab's body swells before the
shell hardens. The crab hides away
until the shell is completely hard.

Dangers

Many crabs do not live very long.
They are eaten by all sorts of
birds, such as seagulls, shags
and cormorants.

Eels, squid, dogfish and big crabs that roam large rockpools also eat small crabs.

Defences

A crab waves its claws to **defend** itself from attack by crabs and other animals. It spreads its legs wide to look bigger and fiercer than it really is.

If a crab loses a claw in a fight,
it can grow a new one.

3-4
years

Adult crab

Once a crab reaches adult size,
it is ready to **mate** and
produce young of its own.

Crab life cycle

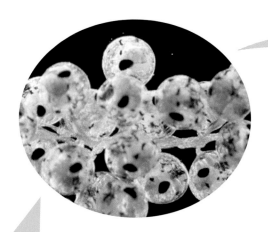

Eggs
The female produces
thousands of eggs.

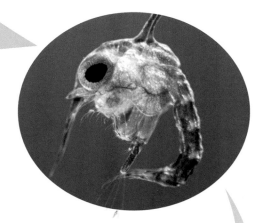

Larva
The eggs hatch
into tiny **larvae** that
float in the sea.

Adult crab
A crab reaches its adult size
after three or four years.

Small crab
The larvae **moult** several times
and become baby crabs.

Glossary

bristles stiff hairs

defend to protect against attack

feeler part of an animal used for touching and smelling

gills special part of animal that helps it to breathe under water

hatch to come out of an egg

jointed made of several parts joined together

larva (plural larvae) the tiny, early stage in a crab's life.

mate when a male and female come together to produce young

moult to cast off an old shell or skin

Index